For Those I Have Loved

KPH

HARP Publishing
The People's Press
Clydesdale, Nova Scotia
Canada

Copyright 2020 © Kyla Heyming

All rights reserved. No part of this book may be used or reproduced
In any manner whatsoever without written permission from the publisher

Information about purchasing this book can be obtained from the publisher:
harppeoplespress@gmail.com
tel 902.863.0396

Catalogue-in-Publication data are on file with Library and Archives Canada

ISBN: 978-0-9938295-9-8

Cover Artist: G. Rodrigue

Graphic Design: Cathy Lin

Printed in Canada by Rapido Books
Published in Canada by HARP The People's Press
216 Clydesdale Road, Clydesdale
Nova Scotia, B2G 2K9, Canada

www.harppublishing.ca

Dedication

For Theodorus Wilhelmus Maria Heyming,

A great man who made me fall in love with stories. My opa taught me that writing and reading were ways to make the world a little wiser and a little more whimsical. He had always wished to have his story told, and so this collection is a homage to his life, and its last few chapters.

This collection is also for those who have lost someone they have cared about, regardless of whether or not life has left them, or if they have left your life. To have had the chance to love at all, is a beautiful blessing we often forget when faced with grief.

In praise of *For Those I Have Loved*

This collection of poems conveys the insight and inner wisdom of an author who is not afraid to walk inside herself and listen to the quiet whispers deep within the recesses of her heart. We are truly given a gift to look into the window of her personal grief and connect to feelings and experiences that are so very relatable. Let's find the courage to follow her lead and take the worthwhile journey of turning inward in order to unlock and attend to our emotions in the most gentle, kind and compassionate way.

Anne Quesnelle, Teacher

So often we cannot describe with words the emotional anguish that one endures after the death of a loved one. As one reads these poetic works, the rawness of grief is effectively conveyed, allowing the reader to grasp a better understanding of the thoughts and feelings that may be experienced during bereavement.

Norm Blanchard, Grief Recovery Specialist

For Those I Have Loved is a sublime elegy for the dead. These naked straightforward poems seek to understand the complexities of grief in its many facets. They are unembellished, humble dedications. The poet's love of those dying or departed is heartbreakingly evident in these poems. Grief and longing tremble in each line of verse. KPH weaves love, sadness, anger, and guilt into an innocent tapestry of remembrance. This is an honest and elegant dedication to the departed; a treasured elegy of verse.

Trisha Cull, Poet of *The Death of Small Creatures*

For Those I Have Loved is an honest, heartfelt, and insightful book about the power of love and loss. Through the lens of her own life, KPH shares with us her vulnerability and courage as she faces losing someone she deeply loves. Her grief is felt, yet through her own personal experiences, she encourages all of us to continue loving.

Dr. Cheryl Bauman, University Professor & Author,
Just Say It: Four Phrases that Will Change Your Life Forever

Table of Contents

For Those I Have Loved 1
Dedication 3
In praise of For Those I Have Loved 4
Prelude 8
For Him 10
Hugs and Thank Yous 11
Alone 12
What They Wanted 13
Someday 14
Angry 15
Cruel Design 16
Surrender 17
Guilty 18
Tell Me the Story 19
Pretty Good 20
End It 21
Teach Him to Find Me 22
A Foolish Dream 23
Eternally 24
Treasure 25
He is Not Weak 26
Stay 27
Seeing Birds 28
Until We Meet Again 29
Box 30
This Life or Another 31
Big Man 32
I'll Remember 33
Legacy 34
For Them 35
Red Railing (for Monique) 36

Theft	*37*
I Wish I Had Paid More Attention (for Oma)	*38*
Keys (for Nellie)	*39*
Grief as Known by the Five Senses	*40*
He was Grief	*41*
Mountain of a Man (for Doris)	*42*
Taken (For Treena)	*43*
For Those I Have Lost	*44*
For Us	*45*
Love in a Lifetime	*46*
Blessed	*47*
Easy	*48*
Empty	*49*
The Youth We Still Long For	*50*
Loosen or Lose It	*51*
Promise	*52*
To Rest	*53*
Poetry & Art	*54*
Losing Me	*55*
Sitting with Sadness	*56*
Five Lessons	*57*
World Ender	*58*
Goodbye	*59*
A Poet's Cure for Mortality	*60*
For Those I Have Loved	*61*
A Word from the Poet	*62*
Acknowledgements	*63*

Prelude

Jamie Anderson said it best: "Grief is just love with no place to go."

The past few years have been a testament to that statement, ever since my family and I were informed that my opa was diagnosed with a fatal condition.

The news came as a shock to me, since I was 22 at the time and had been blessed enough to not have experienced the death of a loved one yet. The first time I had the chance to see my opa after hearing the news, I had been awfully confused. He looked just as cheerful and healthy in his old age as he'd ever been. It was when I got ready to leave him after a wonderful evening together that the gravity of his prognosis crept into my mind.

My opa was a kind and caring man even though he did not appear overly affectionate on the outside. That evening when I put on my shoes and coat to head out, he gave me a hug, told me he loved me, and wouldn't let me go until he truly knew that I knew he loved me. That is when I understood that he was telling me goodbye, whether I wanted to hear it or not.

As time went on, I had the opportunity to spend many more celebrations and occasions with him and my oma. I learned more about my family history, and about his own life. Having survived many hardships, my opa was a man who liked living in the present and looking forward to what the future had to offer. One that was filled with laughter, phone calls on Sunday night, Blue Planet marathons, cooking croquettes and visits to my parents' trailer on the lake to hear the loons sing in the early morning. The past was not really something he preoccupied himself with.

We spent our time together learning, which happened to be one of his absolute favourite things to do. He was always curious about what it was that I did for work, or how my mom would just throw a recipe together and it would taste amazing, or how my dad could build and fix things from scratch, or how my brother managed to figure out any computer program. Even during his very last days, he wanted to learn how to make the pompoms that my oma added to the top of the toques she'd knit. He was a curious mind until the very end, and it kept him happy.

My favourite pastime to do together was to hear and share stories. I got my love of stories from him, and my love of writing from my oma. As non-native English speakers, it was quite funny that English was the only language in which we could communicate with each other. They knew little French, and I knew almost no Dutch. I owe much of my passion for my craft to them for making it so enticing and for encouraging me throughout my pursuit of it.

Neither of them was surprised when I told them that I wanted to make a living off of writing. In fact, they jumped at the chance to be able to read whatever it was that I was writing. My opa became even more intrigued when I started using a typewriter as part of my writing process. Having used one himself in his younger days, he was fascinated by my pull to the machine and how it helped me write some his favourite poetry. It should have come as no surprise to me (though it did at the time) when my opa proposed the idea of having his story written, and by no one other than myself.

That was a moment I would not soon forget, and though both of us had wanted to collaborate on this project together, time and my opa's sickness got the better of us. He was content reading my poetry on Instagram (for which he had created his own account for the sole purpose of staying up to date with my latest poems) and I would take the time to send some others pieces I thought he'd like by email. Though we never did get the chance to work on his story together, I had managed to write a few poems that did just that.

Surely enough, after three years, I had written and composed an entire collection of poems that reflected my thoughts and feelings in regards to the process of learning to grieve for someone, sometimes even before they're gone. As each poem poured out of me and onto the page through my typewriter, I came to understand that grief affects us all, just in different ways. Though a lot of my grief was brought on by death, other forms of it were generated by lost love and even bittersweet partings. Losing my opa little by little over three years allowed me the time to process, understand and work through my emotions in such a way that I was still able to be present with him in his last moments. I wasn't distracted by the prospect of never getting to experience those moments with him again, but rather I enjoyed every bit of those moments.

It was my dream and one of my biggest hopes to have my opa's story told in his lifetime. Even though I wasn't able to write his account of his family's history, I was able to capture some of his last moments, and some of our favourite memories in this collection. I think it was something that both of us wanted to share and cherish together. So much so that only 5 days after I had told him the news that this very collection was to be published, he passed away.

For Those I Have Loved is a collection of grief remembered in love, dedicated to the one man who gave me the courage, and his blessing to share it with the world.

For Him

Hugs and Thank Yous

It started with
a hug and kind
thank yous. I
had taken a trip to
visit and celebrate and
rejoice in the little
amount of
free time
we actually had.
You wrapped your arms
around me and kissed
one cheek, then the other;
then my forehead and
you smiled. You said
 you hadn't been
sold on the idea of a visit
but that now, you were positively
happy. You told me that
you were proud of me. You
told me you loved me and
repeated how happy you were that
I came to visit and
then I felt my
heart tighten. I
smiled. I said I loved you.
I told you I'd make
the trip anytime. You
grabbed my hand and I
squeezed back
saying I'd see you
soon.
Before I made the
trip, Dad had said
that you weren't doing
so good, and part of
me denies it but
the other part felt
that it started
with a hug this
time, and
ended with goodbye.
So next time, hold me
until I let you go
and I'll tell you how
much I love you
because I'm not ready
for goodbye. And now I know
I'll never be.

Alone

He tells me he worries when I'm alone.
He tells me stories of younger days
of loneliness broken by
the company of old friends
in a new world. I smile.
He worries like most, but I am not afraid
to be alone. I'm afraid of loneliness
but it rarely finds me when I am
by myself. It corners me when I am
in the presence of others
who fail to see me as I am.
So, I reassure him. Alone is where
I am at my best, and lonely is but
a test of the spirit.

What They Wanted

He was alive though he
did not want to be. Learning
to grieve before he was gone,
I simply longed for more
time with him. We would talk
and he would cough, and I loved
those little moments nonetheless.
His mind was sharp while
his body was falling apart. Deep in
discussions, I turned to her to ask
her a question and she fell quiet
although I couldn't remember her
speaking. Her eyes darted
around and that's when I found
that my time had been poorly
planned. Her mind was not
withstanding the years
she had lived and I would give
anything now to learn about
her story. Her body intact,
she sat in her chair and knitted
hats she would never wear.
I wanted to learn from them
but they were tired, or away, and
preferred to listen to me instead.
All that I wanted was to know
everything they knew,
knowing all too well there'd be
nothing new to know.

Someday

He will know someday
that his story
is one that is always
worth telling.
He will know someday
that you can't always know
what the future
is foretelling.
He will know someday
that time is a trick
that will never need
magic.
He will know someday
that hope
is the glue that repairs
what is tragic.
He will know someday
that the things he has taught me
will live on
forever.
He will know someday
how I cherished
those days that we would spend
all together.
He will know
one day.

Angry

I'm angry because I was not left alone
to be sad at a time where it was okay
to be sad. I'm sad because I was
preparing myself to lose one person but
was thrown the possibility that I could lose
two. I had to prepare because I went shopping
and bought a dress, only to try it on
at home and think that it was the perfect dress
for a funeral. I had to think because
I've never had to grieve and grief
makes people go mad. I'm mad because
I have drafts of eulogies I read aloud
because I'm afraid of not being able to do it
for real. I'm afraid because I can't be the crutch
for everyone who's loved you and will lose you.
I can't be, because I don't want to be. And I don't
want to be because I'm angry.

Cruel Design

He stares at the clear tubes
coiled on the floor next
to him shaped into
a noose that was meant to
kill him ever so slowly.
I follow his eyes and see
the oxygen lines meant to
keep him with me a little
longer. But sight and seeing
are not the same for every being
and what I would consider
a salvation of time, he contemplates
as cruel design.

Surrender

I tell people you are tired
when they ask how you are doing.
They nod and say things will
get better, and I smile back
knowing they will not. I know
you have an end in sight
despite the fact that you won't
share it with anyone. You are
tired. But you can't get any rest
for once you stop willfully
waking yourself up, life itself
will leave you. You are tired,
and so are we of seeing you
fight a battle your body
has already surrendered.

Guilty

I am guilty of grieving you
before you are even gone. Before
you're even sent to your grave
or we've obtained a death certificate.
Before we've even gotten a call
or a card that sends its condolences.
I am guilty of not saying I Love You
enough though I know you know it.
Of constantly saying things
instead of listening. Of teaching you
my language rather than learning
ours. I am guilty of hoping, waiting
and counting on more time though
everyone knows there will never
be enough of it. Never enough
birthdays and holidays, and brief
rides to Tim Hortons for afternoon
coffee, or games of cards while
listening to classical music. I am
guilty of focusing on where I was
going and forgot to find out
where I came from, because
the prelude makes the story work
and the characters wiser. I am guilty
of all of this much too late, and I pray
that someday, you'll forgive me.

Tell Me the Story

Tell me the story of my past
before you become
nothing more
than a memory.
Tell me the story of why
you had crossed land and sea
to start a new life when the one
you really loved was left behind.
Tell me the story of what
was lost and loved and longed for
before you imagined a future
where you found and loved and gained
everything you now have.
Tell me the story of when
you'd had enough and yet kept trying
despite having already paid your
dues to the world and to a life that
should've been easier.
Tell me the story of who
you wanted to be, and who you are
now, and how regardless of how different
they are, you are proud nonetheless.
Tell me the story of where
you think you'll be, so that I'll
be able to reach out to you
and talk with you a little longer,
feeling as though my time with you
has never been enough.
Tell me the story of our past
so that you'll stay with me
and forever be, so much more
than just a memory.

Pretty Good

He told me that my poem was
pretty good. He also thought
that Van Gogh was an
alright painter. And so, I painted
him into the prettiest
of poems hoping that at least
there he could stay
and that there
I could find him.

End It

The air doesn't seem
to reach his lungs
anymore though
he does not seem
to mind it either.
The tubes from his
oxygen tank are spread
out across their home
like the lines
of a map
that could bring him back
to us. But he is tired
from his journey and
wishes it would end.
He circles around the corners,
a little slower,
a little faster,
a little closer to
the stairs; then
his eyes flicker away
for a moment. He will wait
until there are no passengers
or people passing by
to watch him try
to end it.

Teach Him to Find Me

Could you teach him
how to find me?
You've got a knack for that and for
knowing when I need to hear from you
even when I don't always want
to hear it. So as he approaches his last
sunset and the reality of it all
sinks in, my stomach does backflips
knowing that sooner, rather than later,
I will not be able to see him anymore.
I will not be able to listen to his stories of
the old country, or to hear him laugh
at my ridiculous antics, or to learn
how to make the perfect pizza crust,
croquette, or apple bollen. I am told
that the next time I see him will
most likely be the last time that I see him,
so I organize my thoughts and
I plan our time to a tee. He is too weak
to follow through when that day
comes, so I give him a hug and
I tell him "I Love You". That is all
he has ever needed to know from me.
But please, teach him the trick
that defies the laws of time, and
let him learn how to find me.

A Foolish Dream

My father,
so used to speaking
on the phone,
found himself
getting caught on
every word as he
repeated to his own dad
to hang in there.
He knew that his plea
was a selfish request
but still, he asked
for it. I listened to him
measure out every word,
hoping none
would be too much;
for him to say, and
for his father to hear.
And as I listened to
the love and the sadness
between them, I understood
that as much as we might
try to prepare
our minds and our hearts
for the loss of a loved one,
death leaves us all bare
when it claims those
we care about the most.

Eternally

For half an hour only,
his attention,
his heart,
his world was mine.
We delighted in old stories
and new dreams,
with the possibility of wondering
how butterflies fly.
Sitting at his feet, his voice
became a beautiful sound
only ever whispered,
as though he was confiding in me
life's biggest secret. It was just
half an hour
but it will be a moment
I will remember eternally.

Treasure

You speak only in short huffs, and I talk
in long, extended, eloquent sentences.
I waste precious breath while you
measure yours, preserving what you may
in the hopes that it'll grant you one last
possible moment, or one last memory.
So I talk and you listen, as you wait
to say your last words to me, having taught me
the importance of choosing words wisely.
I share with you as many as I can muster, so
that you may foster the courage to pick
just the right ones and leave. Please know
that whatever you'll say, I will replay
them forever. For though your words
are not gold, they will be treasured.

He is Not Weak

They tiptoed around him,
seeing his fragility as
the inability to move on.
But he is not weak, he is tired.
A man once truly admired for the things
he desired, has now acquired a will
just to leave it.
They hovered around him,
seeing a man in a shell,
stuck in the hell he had built.
But he is not weak, he is kind.
A man easily defined by the life
he refined, has now resigned himself
just to leave it.
They lingered around him,
seeing the light of
his eyes slowly die out.
But he is not weak, he is proud.
A man who readily vowed that the life that
he found, has now been endowed
and can leave it.

Stay

My hands are shaking,
and my ears are ringing,
and my head is hoping,
and my heart is quaking,
and my body's bracing,
and my eyes are closing,
and my mind is racing,
and my voice is breaking,
because you keep
fading away
and there's no better way
to ask you to stay
when we both know
you can't. You've been
aching for so long
that it's time to move on
but I still wished
that you'd stay with me.

Seeing Birds

My mother tells me
that he has started to see
birds
that are not there.
They flutter onto his lap
and sing to him.
I'd like to think that Death
is reminding him of what
he loved about life,
as he gifts him
memories
and hope
during moments where
all he can do
is wait.

Until We Meet Again

I knew that you had died even before
mother called me. She asked me
if I could talk so I hid behind
the storage shelves at work and let her
tell me the news. I cried then, quietly,
as my tears seemed to sympathetically stream
down my face because my mother
could not control her own. So, I cried
when my mother cried, and I didn't want to cry
at work. I left and headed home. I changed
into one of your sweaters and went to the coffee
shop you always took me to
for an apple fritter and black tea. I felt
like I should be crying, or sad, or even a little
upset but all I did was smile as the sun set
and think about what I would tell you
when I'd see you next.

Box

His life was a burden
I never knew
could fit in
so small a box.

This Life or Another

At the celebration of your life, a crowd of odd
and familiar faces filled a room we thought
would be much too big. It was strange
for me to be smiling in a room full of people
who were crying, but my smile stayed.
I guess that's the difference between
those who truly believed that they'd only get
one lifetime with you and those who knew
there'd be more. I still smile to this day
as I think of all of the things I'm going to say
to you; in this life, or the next.

Big Man

The house seemed full for people who kept
so little. Everything was still perfectly placed and
there wasn't any space with dust on it. It was
impeccable though the air was heavy.
He had died peacefully;
that is as peacefully as a man who's been waiting
on death for three years can be. But his breath
finally left him and we got the call. My mother
was organizing herself and her thoughts,
and whatever else we would need before
we even made it to the house. My father was there
but quiet. My brother couldn't stop crying, having
nothing to hide behind anymore; and I just watched
them all as they grieved on their own.
He had been such a big man. His presence
like his height was not something you could
easily miss. Though he is missed now, the house
he made into a home was so much smaller
then I remembered, even without his large stature
overcrowding the doorways, the hallways
and the basement steps. His service had been fine
and while I had tried to prepare as best as I could
for someone who had not faced death yet, I was not
prepared for the small box we were handed at the end.
It was supposed to contain all that he had been and
it baffled me that so big a man could fit in so small a space.
But this modest memento was a sign of life's greater
design that he was no longer on this earth anymore.
The absence of his presence would be felt in
more places than just the doorways, and hallways
and basement steps of the house he once called home.

I'll Remember

I remember our numerous trips to the zoo and the evenings
we'd watch nature shows while eating homemade pizza. I remember
snacking on rainbow marshmallows served in wooden bowls
while Oma played a song on the piano that I knew belonged in
a Western movie. I remember apple picking in the backyard and
listening to you talk about birds. I remember afternoons at Tim Hortons,
any Tim Hortons, with one coffee split between two cups
that you had brought from home, and something sweet to go with it. I
remember classical music from the living room speakers. I remember plaid
shirts tucked-in and your leather slippers. I remember the white budgie and the
yellow budgie and how you had given them both the same name
that sounded like "peaches". I remember the Dutch artwork that looked
like artefacts of a family history you spoke life of. I remember the first
time I saw a picture of you as a young boy in boarding school
and how I thought you looked like a young Macaulay Culkin. I remember
the basement with its orange carpet and cases of wine-making
equipment. I remember the stone fireplace and the Christmas I got
a doll that cried. I remember March Break visits with
curry chicken, card games, lemon pudding and Science North. I
remember afternoon teas and reading "Prince Prunella
and the Purple Peanut." I remember building things, and fixing
things, and the one time you put butter on a door hinge because it kept
creaking. I remember watching home movies and flipping through
photo albums and hoping I could remember those times too. I remember you
explaining to me how to do things the right way, regardless of what
I was doing. I remember learning. I remember you reading the paper,
watching soccer for the sport and the Tour de France for the scenery.
I remember you calling me by my full name just so that you'd get
the chance to say your own daughter's name as well. I remember not
wanting to write down any of this for fear of forgetting them altogether, but
I guess this way, I'll remember your life, and not just how you left it.

Legacy

He left me a legacy
of love,
of curiosity
and of childlike wonder
of a world
that still surprises
the cynical
and graces the good.

For Them

Red Railing (for Monique)

There stands alone
a red railing
that is more
than just that.
It shows me
the way to you. I search
for it when I want answers,
peace and a little hope.
I lean on it
when realizing where I am
is too much, and when knowing
I'll be back sooner
rather than later
leaves me wishing I never knew
it was there to begin with.
Walking next to it,
I am guided by the faith
I have and the connection
we will always
share. It is why
I will return
to where
the red railing rests
and where you
do too.

Theft

She hovers at
the back of my mind
or beside me
but she hovers
close as the moment
nears. I stay
next to him and
talk and talk and
talk relentlessly
so I won't need to face
the reality of him
leaving. She was
my reasons and he
was my way and
today, they are
together and I am
alone.

I Wish I Had Paid More Attention (for Oma)

I wish I had paid more attention when
you played piano. When you taught me
each note and rewarded me with praise
in the form of a phrase in a language
that was foreign to me, or with a treat
from the bowl of many goodies. I wish
I had paid more attention when you
baked cherry squares or custard squares
or any squares for that matter because
the recipes had remained in our family
for generations even though you weren't
the baker in the bunch. I wish I had paid
more attention when you spoke of our family,
our ancestry and the similarities I had
with cousins overseas, who apparently
looked just like me. I wish I had
paid more attention because
this realization has come too late,
and your memory and your mind are slowly
resigning themselves to letting go.

Keys (for Nellie)

Your hands glided over the keys much like mine
do now and somehow, there was music from both.
You don't play the keys anymore, at least
not like before, and though I long for the music,
it's a chore for you. So, I'll type away and hope
you'd replay the tune you knew by heart,
and the song that's part of mine.

Grief as Known by the Five Senses

Grief looks like
two blue eyes and a smile
from quivering lips.
Grief looks like
a sea of black clothing
with pops of uneven colour
made to appear less depressing.
Grief looks like
folded hands, and arms, and
sheets, and napkins, since
no one wants to be open.
Grief sounds like
staggered hums, short sighs,
quick goodbyes and condolences
copy-pasted one after another.
Grief sounds like
ice cave echoes that are not returned.
Grief tastes like
stale sandwiches and burnt coffee
that's been left out for people
who were supposed to show up
but never did.
Grief tastes like
something sour that used to be
sweet but that spoilt sooner
than expected.
Grief smells like
strong perfume, hairspray
and dust.
Grief feels like
cold marble and March mornings.
Grief feels like
tissue paper skin covered
with steel wool, hoping to stay warm.
Grief feels like
guilt over promises that were made
but not kept even though
no one ever expected them to do so.
Grief feels heavy;
with all of this love, and nowhere to leave it.

He was Grief

I had been running from him, but he kept his arms
wide open while his blurred lips turned
into a sympathetic grin. Grief had been waiting
to welcome the sorrows of a relentless
optimist confronted with death for the first time.
Life is rarely easy and death seemed even less so,
but grief would help me get through
what I was convinced I wouldn't survive.

Mountain of a Man (for Doris)

Throughout my life, I have met wild
men and women who were desperately
hoping to tame the thing that
made them interesting, only to
call it progress. But as I roamed the world
to find a home out there, but also in you,
I stumbled upon a mountain of a man
with eyes of thunder and a soul
like the fall. I am sad that his scenery
of a self has faded before I was
able to find a comparable person.
Now the world I know is a little
more dull and a lot less magical.

Taken (For Treena)

Taken too soon
from a world
that wanted nothing
but to embrace you,
you are loved and
missed to this day;
by those who knew you
and by those
who wish they had.

For Those I Have Lost

I had lived for so long
in an enchanting,
blissful
ignorance
where time was abundant
and death
was the paradise
of the believers.
But I was wrong
and I am selfish.
I panicked when I was told
that time was not
endless.
It slipped
through my fingers
and years
became mere moments
trapped in an unreliable memory.
I spent my time
reminiscing about people
who are not yet gone.
I am so sorry
that I've forgotten you
by trying to remember you.

For Us

Love in a Lifetime

Little by little, my memory grows
brittle and though my resolve
is strong, my mind will snap
if it forgets all that it loved
in its lifetime.

Blessed

I believe that my struggles
with grief were brought on
by luck and blessings,
because I have been given
so much that I'd hate to lose it.

Easy

The news came in today
that changed
my heading. I didn't know
that time was blind
to begging. So, we made our way
to say our graces
and blessings; it's hard to say
goodbye
when I'm not ready. So, what's
the point
in saying that days get better
if all I ever hear
are lies that fester? I'll throw
a desperate cry and try
to get her, but all of this
in vain; this pain
won't leave me.
Because loving you was always
easy and losing you
is so damn hard.

Empty

My grief empties me
and I just wished
it would leave me alone.
Then again, should
the pain disappear,
it means you would too.

The Youth We Still Long For

Endings are merely
moments we remember
in light of the life
we've loved and
the youth we still long for.

Loosen or Lose It

I see it coming.
I should be loosening
my grip but instead
it tightens. I hold on
to you because I'd
rather lose myself
before losing you.

Promise

I promise to love you
as best as I can,
for as long as I can,
until time gets
the best of us both.

To Rest

Just give me a moment
to rest my head,
to rest my legs and
to rest in peace.

Poetry & Art

Tell me the story that you've never
told; the one you've held onto
until you grew old. Tell me
the story right from the start
and share all of your memories
so I can turn them into poetry and art.

Losing Me

I've learned to grieve for people
before they're actually gone
because if I hold on for too long,
and life
or love
leaves them before I've said my piece,
there's a greater chance
that the person I loose is me.

Sitting with Sadness

I don't want to smile.
I want to sit with this sadness
until I don't feel it
anymore.
Because loving you was easy,
and losing you is not.

Five Lessons

Time;
ticks by, knowing why,
blink of eye, cease to try
to stop it.
Love;
heart pounds, can't touch the ground,
lost and found, one single bound
to reach it.
Faith;
holy might, seek the light,
crusaders fight, know what's right
to find it.
Truth;
righteous swear, wrong beware,
to heart's compare, chiefs declare
to leave it.
Life;
exciting start, bear the mark,
story sparks, fear the dark
that ends it.

World Ender

Despite everything,
I'll still be there
holding your hand
and whispering
"I love you"
when your world ends,
and mine along with it.

Goodbye

I learned that goodbye
sounds a lot like:
"I wish I could
love you longer
if only I had the time."

A Poet's Cure for Mortality

I wrote you into a poem because I didn't know
how else to cope
with the possibility of losing something
with someone so dear to me.
By putting your name
to the page, you became immortal
for me, and for everyone else
who shared your memory. I could keep
you close when life took you away.

For Those I Have Loved

I am blessed
beyond any reasonable doubt
to have loved
and been loved
by those who refused to think
that love was not limitless.
I was taught to believe
by the greatest believers
that we are only bound
by where our minds
will lead us and
where our courage
will take us.
I hold this great belief
that great love
will not end. It will find
a new home
in memories
and personalities similar
to those that have been lost.
It is the greatest tragedy
of grief;
having so much love
and nowhere to give it.

A Word from the Poet

Losing someone you love, regardless of how close, how sudden, or how peacefully it might happen, is never an easy thing. I hope that these poems can serve as a comfort to you, as an acknowledgment that you are not alone, and as a reminder to think not just on the sad times you are feeling but also on the good times you've had.

As difficult as it might be, remember that your grief is a simple indication that the one you've lost was loved so greatly; that in itself is something to be happy about. Let it be an opportunity for you to heal, to learn, and to grow.

I wish you a peaceful journey through love, loss and learning, as you read my own in "For Those I Have Loved."

Acknowledgements

Thank you dearly Opa for your love and lessons over the years, and your blessing in your last. PB, for being my sounding board, my perpetual editor, my go-to artist, my travel buddy and fellow Northern Wander Woman, but most importantly, for being with me since the very beginning of this dream, and for believing in me every single step of the way.

Maman and Papa, for your never-ending support, not just in regards to my work, but towards any and all projects I throw myself into. Nicholas, for promising to take up reading once more whenever I got published for the first time. Veronique, Marc and Doris Desjardins, the ones who have become like a second family to me, for wanting to celebrate my successes with me, and never letting me forget to be proud of the work I've accomplished.

Jean-Paul Courtemanche and Mariola Musial for their invaluable feedback and editorial skills. The facilitators and participants of the Writing with Care Retreat 2019 in Ochre Pit Cove, NL (Lisa Porter, Lois Brown, Lori Clarke, Dorothy Lander, John Graham-Pole, Priscilla Johnson, Paula Boggs, Trisha Cull and Ingrid Feustel) for accepting me, motivating me, and encouraging me to continue to share my writing with the world because I have something to say, and it is worth hearing.

Monique, for being my guardian angel and reminding me of all the things I have to be grateful for. Harp Publishing: The People's Press, for making a reality of a dream that's been 12 years in the making. The numerous writers and poets I've been inspired by, for lending me your voices until I could discover my own.

My reliable typewriter Hank, for providing me with a most beautiful outlet that has saved my life, and that's preserved so many others. My family and friends who witnessed me work throughout the years to accomplish what I had set my mind to. Those who continue to read and follow my poetry, for your support and patronage.

And, for those I have loved, for making this possible.

www.ingramcontent.com/pod-product-compliance
Lightning Source LLC
Chambersburg PA
CBHW061145010526
44118CB00026B/2881